PROCRASTINATION

7 Steps to Beat Procrastination And Increase Your Productivity

TABLE OF CONTENTS

should thus be thought of as universal. As befitting its nature, it is presented without assurance regarding its prolonged validity or interim quality. Trademarks that are mentioned are done without written consent and can in no way be considered an endorsement from the trademark holder.

INTRODUCTION

This book contains useful and accurate information on procrastination and the techniques that you can use to overcome it.

Procrastination may seem trivial, but it can actually have a significant impact on your life. If you keep delaying tasks or postponing events, your personal, professional, and social lives may suffer.

Fortunately, there are ways on how to overcome procrastination. It can be difficult to achieve this, but it is not impossible. You just have to believe in your own abilities and never give up.

In this book, you will learn about the strategies and methods that you can use to successfully get things done and achieve your goals. You will see examples and read about studies that back up the theories discussed in the chapters.

You will learn about the exercises that you can do to boost your productivity and fight procrastination. Don't worry because there are step by step instructions provided to guide you all the way.

You will learn how to set goals as well as how to practice visualization to have the kind of life that you dream of. You will also learn how to take action and how to manage your time wisely.

This book contains all the fundamentals that you have to know. So, what are you still waiting for? Get started with the first chapter and begin your journey towards a life of productivity, happiness, and success.

Thanks for downloading this book, I hope you enjoy it!

CHAPTER 1

WHY DO PEOPLE PROCRASTINATE?

Procrastination happens to everyone. However, some people procrastinate to the point that they experience a downward spiral. This is obviously not something that you want to happen to you.

What Is Procrastination?

Procrastination refers to the action of postponing or delaying something. Elizabeth Gilbert claimed that all procrastination is fear and Steven Pressfield called it the resistance to begin difficult work.

Christine Li, a clinical psychologist, agreed that procrastination is typically caused by conflict or fear. So, even though you feel motivated to do something, your fear of stress, failure, or criticism may get the best of you and cause you to harbor negative thoughts. You may start to doubt yourself, causing you to stop before you even start.

When people procrastinate, they may be fearful of not being able to remain focused. They may be fearful of having to give up or they may want to escape to something easier. They may have a lot of fears. Moreover, their procrastination may be due to a variety of factors.

Common Causes of Procrastination

There are a lot of various reasons why people procrastinate.

Laziness

This is perhaps the most common association with procrastination. When people procrastinate, they are often labeled as lazy. Lazy people tend to think that they have a lot of time to do their task. They also tend to believe that they have enough energy for it. Thus, they do not prioritize it and usually end up having to rush finishing it. They also often lack the energy needed for the task because they already spent all their energy doing the less important things.

For example, a man who has to mow the lawn may feel lazy and put off his task. He may reason out that he has all day to do it. So, he opts to watch TV and take a nap. When he wakes up, he may find that it is already dark and he wasted the entire day not doing anything productive.

Boredom

When people are bored or do not have much interest on a certain topic or activity, they tend to lose focus and do something else. They put off doing their task until the last minute because it does not make them feel happy, satisfied, or excited.

For example, a student who lacks interest in mathematics may put off doing her Algebra homework. Instead of starting it, she might watch TV or log on to social media. Likewise, she might cram studying for a test.

Inability to Make Decisions

People who cannot make decisions quickly tend to experience dynamic inconsistency. They often have different versions of themselves at different points throughout their lives. These versions represent their decision-making selves at the moment.

Then again, if their preferences do not align, there could be inconsistencies and unpredictability factors.

For example, a student may wish for an exam to be postponed so that he may have more time to study. He may even be willing to do anything just to have it postponed for another day.

This same student, however, may feel differently a few months before the exam. Since there is a lot of time to prepare, he may not feel any urgency to study. He will not wish for the exam to be postponed and he will not panic at the amount of time left for him to prepare.

This example shows the same decision that is made in different situations. It is true that decisions can change as well as be influenced by present situations. Time inconsistency is a form of dynamic inconsistency. The results of decisions can significantly affect the way people think. Also, people can have different decisions about their immediate and faraway future.

Perfectionism

Some people worry about exposing their weakness and making mistakes. This causes them to put off vital tasks for another day. Such type of mindset was discussed in Mindset: The New Psychology of Success by Dr. Carol Dwick, a psychologist at Stanford University.

In her book, she talked about the power of the mind and how your mindset can affect your success at work, school, and other areas of life. She also stated that people either have a growth mindset or a fixed mindset. Those who have a fixed mindset generally believe that they have limited abilities. Thus, they merely focus on their current talents or intelligence. They do not believe that they can develop new ones. They also believe that talent does not require effort.

Having a fixed mindset is actually dangerous because it can hinder your ability to learn, grow, and make positive changes. On the contrary, having a growth mindset is healthy. It allows you to believe that your abilities can improve and be developed through hard work and dedication.

People with a growth mindset believe that their talents and brains are merely starting points. They are aware of their innate strengths as well as their potential to achieve more accomplishments. Their growth mindset motivates them to learn more as well as overcome challenges to reach success.

According to Dwick, your mindset determines your success rate. Those who have the right mindset can lead, teach, and motivate in ways that can make positive changes in their lives as well as of others.

Hillary Rettig, author of The 7 Secrets of the Prolific: The Definitive Guide to Overcoming Procrastination, Perfectionism, and Writer's Block, said that those who procrastinate because of perfectionism usually have a fixed mindset. They avoid performing tasks due to the fear of making a mistake, failing, or seeming imperfect.

A lot of people have the misconception that perfectionism is a good trait. The truth is that it is detrimental and dangerous. It typically involves attitudes and habits that are anti-productive. It also limits the opportunities for success because of unrealistic standards.

Feeling of Overwhelm

It is easy to feel overwhelmed whenever faced with tasks that are too difficult or massive. This can cause a tendency to procrastinate. People who feel overwhelmed typically get a feeling of uncertainty and confusion. They cannot seem to figure out how they should begin the task.

It can truly be difficult to work on a huge project due to the amount of time and effort it requires to finish. Also, you may have to give up certain things just to get the work done. Because of this, you may lose motivation and choose to put off doing the project.

When people become protective of their time, they may practice delay discounting. It is when they choose their personal time over their goals or money. In a study, it was found that people consider getting $85 at the moment for a project the same as getting $100 a few months later for the same project. This proves that a lot of people are willing to lose $17 if they can get paid right away.

Another reason why people procrastinate is time inconsistency. It refers to the notion that a leader may come up with a policy that causes people to make commitments, with the belief that such rule will remain in place. This leader may change the policy later once the commitments are already fulfilled.

For example, a teacher may tell the class that they would have an exam the following Wednesday. Thus, the students all study in preparation for this exam. When Wednesday arrives, the teacher cancels the exam.

In this example, the exam is not really necessary. However, the teacher's announcement was beneficial to the students because they were prompted to study. Thus, they are prepared to learn more and they can prepare better for the exam once it occurs.

In a study done at Stanford University, it was found that time inconsistency is a huge factor in individual work. It is common for people to have a present bias when they work on tasks that they can fully control. They tend to value their present time more than future results because the human brain generally values immediate rewards more than future rewards.

A study on delayed gratification was done by Walter Mischel along with a team of researchers at Stanford University. It involved children who were given the option to receive one reward immediately or two rewards after fifteen minutes.

Mischel and his team continued to study the children as they grew older. They found that those who opted to wait longer to receive two rewards were able to achieve more success. On the other hand, those who opted to receive their reward right away were found to have lower educational attainment, more behavioral problems, and higher BMIs.

Lack of Motivation

People who lack motivation also have a tendency to procrastinate. They are prone to staying stuck or becoming idle. They may even think that there is something wrong with them when they are not able to do simple tasks. These people are not in the right state of mind, which is why they cannot find solutions to even the most basic problems.

In a study conducted at Carnegie Melon University, it was found that individuals lack motivation when they see little value in the potential results of their work. Nevertheless, when they are able to see clearly how their work is related to their goals, concerns, and interest, they will be more likely to stay motivated as well as value their work.

In another study published in The National Academics of Sciences, Engineering, and Medicine, it was found that motivation consists of goal choice and self-confidence.

Self-confidence does not really produce motivation, but it can help people judge their own capabilities. Hence, it is regarded as part of a bigger concept of motivation for achieving ultimate goals.

Skill Deficit

People who lack the necessary skills to do a task may also procrastinate because they either do not know how to start or do not have the capability to carry out the task. For example, students who are slow readers may put off studying for a test. They may even refuse to read even though they are already pressed for time.

Fear of the Unknown

There is a saying that what you do not know cannot hurt you. However, this saying is not true. In most cases, ignoring something for a long time can only makes things worse.

For example, if you notice an unusual mole on your shoulder one day, you may begin to panic. You may jump into conclusions, such as the mole being cancerous. The fear of having cancer may cause you to procrastinate and avoid going to a doctor for medical assessment. You may simply hope that the mole will disappear on its own.

This is a classic example of the fear of the unknown. Most people do not want to know the truth because it might be devastating. However, it is so much better to know the truth, even if it is not what you want to hear.

In a study done by researchers at the University of Michigan, it was found that letting misinformation linger in your mind can be detrimental to your mental health. If you allow it to remain in your memory, it will continue to influence your thinking.

In addition, the researchers found that personal views and beliefs can become huge obstacles for correcting misinformation. In fact, attempting to present facts to a person who has been misinformed can backfire. If this person does not like the truth, his incorrect ideas may even be amplified.

Keep in mind that when it comes to health, ignoring problems instead of finding out the truth can result in worse conditions or even death. Ignorance is not always bliss. Knowledge is actually power.

The "I will do it later" Habit

This habit encourages procrastination as it gives the reason that tasks can be done on a later schedule. People who have this habit think that they can carry out their tasks later or tomorrow. They continue to put off finishing their tasks until they realize that they have little to no time left.

Also, those who have this habit typically have an unrealistic point of view. For example, they may have ideals such as being able to have a lot of energy, workout regularly, and have a healthy diet. In reality, however, they are exhausted, unmotivated, and undisciplined.

This phenomenon is related to a couple of concepts: dynamic inconsistency and hot and cold empathy gap.

The hot and cold empathy gap pertains to the state of mind that causes individuals to underestimate the effects of their instinctive drive towards their preferences, attitudes, and behaviors. Its most vital aspect is that human understanding hugely depends on their state of mind.

Say, you are angry at the moment. Your current state prevents you from imagining yourself as a calm person. Likewise, if you are hungry, you may not be able to imagine that you are full.

Dynamic inconsistency refers to the situation in which the preferences of the decision maker change and become inconsistent over time. This shows that a person can have different versions of himself when it comes to making decisions. Every one of these versions represents him at different points in his life. Inconsistencies occur when his preferences do not align.

Distraction

Today, there are numerous things that can distract you; social media, television, gossip, e-mail, and text messages are only some of them.

In a survey done by Career Builder, it was found that one in five employers think that their employees only spend a maximum of five hours per day on productive work. They also said that these employees often engage in office gossip as well as constantly use the Internet and their smartphones.

Anxiety

Anxiety can cause procrastination. For example, people may procrastinate when their working memory gets overwhelmed or when they overestimate the amount of tasks they can finish in a certain timeframe. They may also procrastinate when they have an all or nothing thinking or unrelated standards as well as when they always expect a negative outcome.

Furthermore, they may procrastinate when they have an uneven cognitive profile or when they experience difficulties with cognitive skills such as planning, sequencing, or initiating.

People may have different reasons why they procrastinate. Oftentimes, they even mix and match the causes discussed above. Nevertheless, whatever their reasons are, they can still overcome procrastination by taking the necessary actions, which will be covered in the succeeding chapters.

CHAPTER 2

PRACTICAL EXERCISES TO STOP PROCRASTINATION

There are plenty of exercises you can do to stop procrastination. According to psychologists, whichever exercise you choose, you have to be kind towards yourself.

Tony Stubblebine, a leadership coach, adds that you have to practice meditation to strengthen your focus. This way, you can control your fear of failure, guilt, and perfectionism, which often leads to procrastination.

People are generally controlled by their subconscious worries and thoughts. Through meditation, they can gain more control over their mind. Once you awaken your rational brain, you can focus more on the important things. Also, through meditation, you can train your focus and avoid paralysis.

Meditation Exercise

Here is the meditation exercise that Stubblebine recommends:

Step 1. Close your eyes.

Step 2. Begin to count your breath. Aim for 50 breaths. This can last between five and ten minutes.

Step 3. Be mindful of the activities of your mind. It is common for the human mind to wander during meditation. When this happens, you should make a mental note of the thoughts that come to your mind.

Step 4. Use the following format when making a mental note of your thoughts: "I am aware that I am + verb." For example, if a thought about work suddenly crosses your mind, you can say "I am aware that I am thinking about writing e-mails to clients."

Step 5. Once you are done taking note of your distracting thoughts, you should go back to counting your breath.

Motivation Exercise

When people lack motivation, it can be difficult for them to get anything started. This simple motivation exercise can help you deal with this problem:

Step 1. Sit down comfortably.

Step 2. Visualize starting the task.

Step 3. Visualize every step of the task.

Step 4. Repeat steps 1 to 3.

One-minute Exercise

This exercise is straightforward and simple. In one minute, you have to prepare yourself to do the task that you have been putting off. Once you get started, you should keep going. Refrain from taking a break or doing anything else. Do not stop until you have finished it.

For example, if you have to write a book but you have been procrastinating for a week, you can do this exercise. Sit down in front of your computer, open your file, and start typing. Do not stop writing your book until it is done. If you focus on this task, you will not be distracted by other things such as phone calls, social media, text messages, computer games, or e-mails.

Instant Pause and Reset: Label and Let It Be

This exercise was popularized by Jillian Pransky, a restorative yoga instructor. To do it, you have to do the following:

Step 1. Pause to reset your attention. Take some time to observe the workings of your body and mind. If you find your mind wandering, simply bring it back to the present moment.

Step 2. Pause to sense where your body meets the ground. Allow your face, shoulders, and neck to relax.

Step 3. Observe the way your body and mind work. Put a label on your thoughts and feelings.

Step 4. Bring your focus to your next three breaths. As you breathe in, mentally chant "I am". As you breathe out, mentally chant "here now".

Step 5. Pause at the end of your third breath. Observe the way your body gives you support. Open up your awareness towards your surroundings.

Feel Good Technique

Negative thoughts are instant productivity killers. When you think of negative thoughts, your motivation can immediately decline. Thus, you should make it a habit to have positive thoughts. Replace negative thoughts with positive ones.

Step 1. Identify a task that you consider to be unpleasant.

Step 2. Think of the positive sides of this task. For example, you may put off cleaning your room because it is tiresome and boring. Instead of thinking of it this way, you can think of the benefits you can get from it, such as having a cleaner environment and exercising your body.

Step 3. Give yourself a reward once you finished the task. This way, you can look forward to something good.

CHAPTER 3

PRACTICAL EXERCISES TO BOOST PRODUCTIVITY

Numerous studies have shown that exercise can increase productivity. Essentially, the fitter and healthier you are, the more productive you can be. If you have a hectic schedule, don't worry because you can still exercise. Also, there is no need for you to buy expensive tools or equipment to exercise for increasing productivity.

Physical Exercises You Can Do at Work

The following exercises are ideal for people who spend most of their time in the office. They are recommended by Shruti Bangera, a senior subject matter expert on Physiotherapy at Portea Medical. These exercises are simple, easy, and do not require complex equipment. You can quickly do them during your break time.

Seated Leg Raiser

This exercise can strengthen your core muscles and help reduce back pain. It is also barely noticeable under a desk.

Step 1. As you sit in your chair, straighten your leg and hold it in place for at least five seconds. You can straighten one leg at a time or both legs at the same time.

Step 2. Lower your legs back to the floor, but do not let your feet touch it.

Step 3. Repeat steps 1 and 2 fifteen times. Alternate your legs if you choose to raise them individually.

Silent Seat Squeeze

This isometric glutes exercise is low-key yet effective. It can tone your buttocks and strengthen your glutes.

Step 1. Squeeze your buttocks for five to ten seconds. Release.

Step 2. Repeat step 1 until your glutes get tired.

Fab Abs Squeeze

It strengthens the abs as well as the sides of the stomach. It can be done as you walk around the office or sit down on your desk.

Step 1. Take a deep breath. Tighten your abdominal muscles and bring them inwards as you breathe out.

Step 2. Hold your squeezed position for five to ten seconds. Release.

Step 3. Do twelve to fifteen repetitions.

Shoulder Shrug

It strengthens the shoulder muscles as well as reduces the pain that is caused by constant computer work.

Step 1. Raise your shoulders up to your ears. Hold the position for five seconds. Relax.

Step 2. Do fifteen repetitions.

Step 3. Get two paper reams. Hold a paper ream in each one of your hands. Stand up and perform the shoulder shrug exercise.

Mental Exercises for Increasing Focus and Productivity

According to research, the average attention span has decreased by 30% since 2000 – that's roughly only eight seconds. Today, you have to quickly master and adapt new applications and skills much faster. Keep in mind that concentration is critical to accomplish more with less. The following mental exercises can help you improve your focus as well as productivity:

Little Wins

Researchers have found that people tend to rekindle their childhood creativity and curiosity by focusing on small details. These small steps quickly add up and allow them to accomplish greater things in life.

Step 1. Find something small or simple that you can focus on. For example, you can choose to read an article or outline a project. Set a realistic timeframe for it.

Step 2. Focus on it for eight seconds or one minute. You can go as long as five minutes if you can. Make sure that you do not get distracted or take a break. Completely devote yourself to engaging in this task.

Step 3. Give yourself a break when you are done with the task or once you reached ninety minutes.

The key requirement for this exercise is self-discipline. You have to discipline yourself to stay away from distractions. You can go to a place where you cannot be disturbed by other people. You can also turn off your phone, deactivate your social media accounts, or mute your notifications. Refrain from giving in to the urge to check your e-mail or phone.

Candle Gaze

This exercise stimulates your pineal gland by making you focus on light.

Step 1. Go to a dark room and light a candle.

Step 2. Get a chair and place it six feet away from the candle. Sit down.

Step 3. Stare at the soft flickering light of the candle. Refrain from thinking about anything else. Do this for five minutes.

Mirror Motivation

Eye contact is an incredibly rewarding form of concentration. When you make eye contact and form a deep connection with someone else, you experience a moment of Zen. The cells in your body radiate peace and confidence during this moment.

Step 1. Stand in front of a mirror and make a couple of marks on your eye level. Visualize them as a pair of human eyes that stare back at you.

Step 2. Focus on keeping your head still. Refrain from having any other thoughts.

Step 3. Keep your eyes, body, and head still. Believe that you look like a confident and reliable person.

Step 4. Practice deep breathing. Inhale through your nose and exhale through your mouth.

Concentrated Counting

Counting is a form of therapeutic concentration that boosts your ability to lose yourself in a task as well as improves your basic mental elasticity when you quantify meaningful symbols like words or symbols.

Step 1. Get a magazine and flip through the pages. Stop at a random page.

Step 2. On this page, look at the first paragraph and see how many words it has. Count the words again to ensure that you got the correct number.

Step 3. Move on to the second paragraph. Count the words it contains. Add this number to the number you counted from the first paragraph.

Step 4. Move on to the next paragraphs. Do the same thing – count the words and add their number to the previous ones.

Step 5. Stop once you have counted all the words on the page.

Additional Exercises

Here are more exercises you can do:

Eat the Frog First

The idea behind this exercise is to eliminate the biggest and most difficult hurdle first. This way, you can get on with your day without worrying about the challenging tasks anymore. Hence, you will be able to focus on other things.

Step 1. Write down all the tasks that you have to finish before the day ends.

Step 2. Arrange your list of tasks according to priority and difficulty. The ones that are most difficult, urgent, and important should be at the top of your list.

Step 3. Start doing the first task. Do not stop until you have finished it.

Step 4. When you are done with the first task, you should take a short break and then move on to the second task.

Step 5. Continue doing the difficult tasks until you are only left with the easy ones.

Elimination

You may have to eliminate certain tasks on your to-do lists to be more productive. These tasks may either be delegated to someone else or eliminated completely.

Step 1. Write down all your tasks for the day. Evaluate them and determine the ones that absolutely have to be done.

Step 2. Re-evaluate your list and identify the tasks that you can delegate or put off doing for another time. Cross out these tasks from your to-do list. For example, if you have four meetings on your list, you may reduce them to just two. You can send a representative to attend the other two meetings instead.

Step 3. Now, your list should only consist of the tasks that you have to do today no matter what. For example, you may have to attend a very important meeting with a client.

Getting Things Done Approach

It is ideal to be done when you are not clear about how to get things started. It breaks down a complex task into several smaller tasks.

Step 1. Recall your tasks and write them down.

Step 2. Identify and do the actions that need to be done immediately.

Step 3. Organize your tasks.

Step 4. Review the breakdown of tasks.

Step 5. Complete each one of your tasks.

If you want, you can also turn your list into a checklist. Check off the tasks that you have already completed to stay on track.

Do the First Five Minutes of It

The initial five minutes is crucial when doing a task. It gives you a boost and gets you going. According to

Julia Moeller, a post-doctoral research associate, starting a task for five minutes lets you diminish your fears. Once you start something for five minutes, you will be inclined to finish its entirety because you will realize that you can do it and you have control over it.

Step 1. Identify a task that you have been putting off doing.

Step 2. Get a timer and set it to five minutes.

Step 3. Start doing the task. Do not take a break. Eventually, your timer will go off, signaling that five minutes are up. Continue doing the task until it is finished.

The Pomodoro Technique

Francesco Cirillo, an entrepreneur and author, developed the Pomodoro Technique in the 1990's. It was named after the tomato-shaped timer that he used for work. The idea behind this technique is simple: each time you are faced with a difficult task, you have to break it down into timed intervals with short breaks or "pomodoros". This way, you can train your brain to concentrate on your task for short periods of time. This will allow you to meet your deadlines and improve your attention span.

Step 1. Choose a task that you find difficult. For example, you may have to write a book with ten chapters.

Step 2. Get a timer and set it to twenty-five minutes.

Step 3. Start writing the first chapter of your book. When your timer goes off, you can take a break.

Step 4. Go back to writing your book. When your timer goes off again after twenty-five minutes, you can take another break before resuming your work.

Step 5. Keep doing your work until your timer goes off for the fourth time. When this happens, you can increase the duration of your break from five minutes to fifteen minutes or more. You may increase your break time after every four pomodoros to increase your relaxation and productivity.

Time Chunking Method

It is about grouping or splitting tasks so that they can be more bearable and easier to finish. It is similar to the Pomodoro Technique, except that it does not have fixed timeframes for the tasks.

Step 1. Identify your task and split it into chunks. For example, you have to attend a meeting at 9 AM. So, you have to get to the office a few minutes earlier.

Step 2. Start the first chunk of the task. For example, you have to leave your house at 8 AM and drive to work for forty-five minutes.

Step 3. Continue to do this task without any interruption. For example, you have to keep driving. Do not make a stop at a coffee shop to get bagels and coffee. Do not pull over to the side of the road to make a quick phone call. Just keep on driving.

Step 4. Take a short break. Once you have completed the first chunk of the task, you can give yourself a break to rest your body and mind as well as to prepare for the next chunk. For example, once you reach the office at 8:45 AM, you can grab a quick breakfast for fifteen minutes or prepare your presentation.

Step 5. Resume doing the task. Complete the rest of the chunks until you have finished the entire task.

CHAPTER 4

HOW TO SET GOALS

Setting goals is crucial for a brighter future. When you set goals, you are able to determine where you want to go in life, what you want to achieve, and which areas you have to focus on. You are also able to quickly identify distractions so that you can avoid them.

Successful people have goals. These goals give them both short term motivation and long term vision. Such goals also focus their knowledge acquisition and help them organize their resources and time so that they can make the most of everything in life.

You, too, can be successful if you set sharp and clearly defined goals. Your goals will enable you to measure your achievement and take pride in them. You will also be able to see your progress and increase your self-confidence. You will be able to recognize your own competence and ability to achieve your goals.

How to Set Personal Goals

Setting personals goals consists of three levels: creating a big picture, breaking it down into smaller pictures, and executing your plan to achieve your goal. You have to figure out what you want to achieve in the next ten years of your life and work your way towards it.

However, you should also have short-term goals so that you can achieve this long-term goal. For instance, you can also determine what you want to happen in the next five years. Identify your goals for today, tomorrow, next week, next month, and next year as well.

Step 1. Set your lifetime goals.

When you set personal goals, see to it that you find out what you want to do with your life first. What do you hope to accomplish within the next few years? Setting your lifetime goals enables you to gain a perspective that shapes the other areas of your decision making.

For example, in order for you to have a balanced coverage of every vital aspect of your life, you should set goals in the following categories:

a. career – what do you want to attain in your career? What level do you expect to reach?

b. finances – what is the connection between your finances and career objectives? How much money do you want to make in the different stages of your life?

c. education – what kind of skills and knowledge do you need to have to achieve your goals? Are there any particular knowledge or skills that you wish to acquire?

d. family – What do you want to happen in your family life? Do you wish to become a parent? If so, how do you think you can be a good parent? What kind of parent do you want other people, including your relatives and partner, to perceive you?

e. artistic – Do you wish to attain any artistic objectives?

f. attitude – Are you being held back by your mindset? Are you made upset by your behavior? If so, you should set goals to improve your behaviors as well as search for solutions to your problems.

g. physical – Do you have any athletic goals that you wish to attain? Do you hope to be in good physical and mental health when you reach old age? If so, what are the steps that you plan to take in order to achieve this?

h. public service – Do you wish to make the world a much better place to live in? If so, how can you make this happen? What contributions can you make?

i. pleasure – In order to have a happy and satisfying life, you also need to enjoy yourself once in a while. So, how can you do this?

Take a moment to think about your plans. Brainstorm and dig deeper into your life. Choose at least one goal in every category that best reflects what you want to happen or plan to do. Narrow down your choices by reevaluating your answers further. Focus on the goals that are left with you.

See to it that your goals are personal. Do not create goals for other people. Keep in mind that you have to do this for yourself, not for your partner, parents, relatives, friends, or peers. Do not create any goal that would please other people, such as employers or customers, but not yourself. You may consider what your loved ones might think or feel, but ultimately, you have to make a decision that would benefit yourself the most.

You may want to create a personal mission statement too. This way, you can have a sharper focus on your most important goals and turn them into realities as soon as possible.

Step 2. Set smaller goals.

When you are done setting your lifetime goals, you should come up with a five-year plan that consists of the smaller goals that you hope to achieve. These smaller goals should be relevant to your bigger plans in life.

Ideally, you should create a one-month plan, six-month plan, and one-year plan. These plans will help you get closer to your bigger goal. See to it that all your small plans are interrelated so that you will not have a hard time transitioning.

You also have to create a to-do list. It should contain the tasks that you have to do at the moment in order to reach your lifetime objectives. For example, your smaller goal may be to read more books and gain more knowledge that you can use to achieve your bigger goal. At this stage, you can improve the realism and quality of your goal setting.

Furthermore, you have to reevaluate your plans. See to it that they match the ways that you hope to live your life.

Stay on the Right Track

Once you have identified your initial goals, you have to continue the process by updating and reviewing your to-do list daily. You also have to review your long term plans periodically so that you can modify them accordingly. They should reflect your changing experiences and priorities. For example, you can schedule repeating and regular reviews using an online journal.

SMART Goals

SMART stands for:

S – Significant or Specific

M – Meaningful or Measurable

A – Action-Oriented or Attainable

R – Rewarding or Relevant

T – Trackable or Time-Bound

For example, instead of saying that you want "to travel the world", you should say that you hope "to complete your trip to every country in the world by December 31, 2030". Saying that you want to travel the world is vague and does not really point to a specific target date. This can be confusing and might cause you to procrastinate.

However, when you say that you want to visit all countries and complete your journey on or before December 31, 2030, you give yourself a push to the right direction. It also motivates you to prepare for your trip as well as document your journey to seal memories.

Additional Pointers on How to Set Goals

Here are some more tips on how you can effectively set goals and live a more fulfilling life:

State your goals as positive statements.

When you say your goals, you have to say them in a positive manner. Refrain from using words that are associated with negativity such as "don't" and "can't". For example, instead of saying that you "do not want to make stupid mistakes", you can say that you "want to execute your strategies well".

Be precise.

Make sure that your goals are precise. Include time, date, quantity, and other vital information that are relevant to achieving it. This will let you know exactly when you have already attained your goals. Hence, you will be able to feel satisfaction.

Set your priorities straight.

If you have multiple goals, you have to give every one of them a priority. This way, you can avoid getting overwhelmed. Having so many goals can overwhelm and confuse a person. When you set your priorities, you can focus your attention to the goals that matter the most.

Write down your goals.

When you write down your goals, you crystallize them as well as give them more force.

Keep your operational goals simple.

You should have low level goals that are achievable and small. If your goals are too large, you may have a hard time getting progress. On the other hand, keeping your goals incremental and small can give you more reward opportunities.

Set performance goals instead of outcome goals.

When you aim for excellence, success will follow. So, instead of planning for a great outcome, you should plan to have a great journey. Make sure that your journey towards your end goal is fulfilling and an opportunity for learning and growth.

In addition, you should be careful when setting goals that do not give you full control. Keep in mind that instances may occur that are outside of your control. You may be devastated if you do not achieve a goal because of these instances.

For example, if you are in a business, you may encounter an unexpected effect of a government policy. You may also be in a bad business environment. If you are in the sports industry, you may encounter bad luck, suffer from injury, experience poor judgment, or be stuck in bad weather.

However, if your goals are based on your personal performance, you can easily control the way you think and feel about your achievements. You will be able to feel satisfied regardless of the outcome.

Set goals that are realistic.

When you set goals, see to it that you can actually achieve them. Otherwise, you may suffer from unpleasant consequences. Before you make a final decision with regard to committing to doing something, you have to think it over a few times. Refrain from making a decision when you have strong emotions, such as too much happiness, anger, or sadness.

Study the timeline of the goals that you set and determine if you can really stick with it. In addition, you have to factor in the obstacles and challenges that may suddenly come your way. Figure out if you also have to develop certain skills to overcome these obstacles and reach a certain level of growth.

Things to Remember About Achieving Goals

Once you have achieved a certain goal, you have to enjoy the satisfaction that the experience has brought you. Observe how much progress you have also made towards your other goals. If you have achieved a significant goal, make sure that you reward yourself to retain your levels of self-confidence and motivation.

However, if you found your journey to be too easy, you should make your next goal more difficult to attain. On the contrary, if your goal took too much time and effort to be achieved, you should make your next goal a bit easier. If you saw any deficit in your skills in spite of achieving your goal, you have to decide if you want to set a goal that can fix this.

A Practical Example on Setting Personal Goals

By this time, you should already have ample knowledge on how to set goals. To help you apply the theories that you have learned into your own life, you can use the following example as a guide:

Jane works as a writer for a magazine company. She contributes articles and also does some editing work. Since the New Year is fast approaching, she has decided to create some goals for herself:

a. career – She hopes to become the managing editor for the magazine.

b. physical – She wants to be able to run a marathon.

c. artistic – She aims to continue working on her drawings so that she can eventually have an art exhibit.

Jane wrote down her lifetime goals. Afterwards, she broke them down into smaller, more manageable, and easier to achieve goals.

- In a week, she plans to have a meeting with the current managing editor of the company she works for.

- In a month, she plans to speak with the managing editor to find out which skills she needs to hone in order to get the job that she wants.

- In six months, she plans to go back to college and finally earn her degree in journalism.

- In one year, she plans to volunteer for the projects that the managing editor handles.

- In five years, she hopes to become the deputy editor.

Breaking down a huge goal into smaller ones can make it easier for you to accomplish them. See to it that you use the techniques discussed previously so that you can get the results that you want.

Take note that if you want to succeed in life, you have to set goals for yourself. Without goals, you will lack direction and focus. Through goal setting, you can take control of your life. You also get a benchmark for identifying whether or not you are actually making progress. Furthermore, keep in mind that goal setting begins with mindful consideration of what you hope to accomplish. It also ends with tons of hard work and efforts.

CHAPTER 5

CASE STUDIES OF GREAT PERFORMERS

A study conducted at Princeton University focused on finding out what happens to the brains of the subjects when they make choices between getting a large reward at a later time and getting a small reward right away.

The researchers have found that the brain has two areas for controlling behavior. These areas actually compete with each other whenever the person tries to make a decision between long term goals and short term ones.

The researchers turned to an economic dilemma in which consumers become impatient during the present moment and yet plan to be patient at a later time. For instance, a person is given the option to receive $10 tomorrow and $9 today. Since a lot of people are inclined to give in to immediate rewards, this person is likely to choose the $9.

On the other hand, if this person is asked if he would rather receive $9 after one year or $10 after one year and one day, he would most likely choose the $10. Both options are not immediate, so the person is more inclined to choose the bigger reward even though it is a little delayed.

This study on procrastination focused on fourteen students from Princeton University. Their brains were scanned as they considered delayed reward options. Once, they were offered Amazon.com gift cards that cost $5 to $40. They were told that they can get these gift cards right away. However, they can receive a bigger amount if they wait for two to six weeks.

It was found that when these students considered choices that involved the possibility of immediate rewards, certain areas of their brain were activated. These are the areas that get affected by the neural systems related to emotions. In addition, the decisions that they made activated their brains systems that were connected to abstract reasoning.

The researchers also found that when the students were given the option to choose a short term reward and yet they went for a bigger long term reward, the calculating areas of their brain became more active than the emotional areas. However, when they opted for the short term reward, the activities of both areas were found to be nearly identical, except that the emotional area had a little more activity.

After the study, the researchers concluded that choosing short term rewards can activate the areas of the brain that are related to emotions as well as overcome the areas that are related to abstract reasoning.

Moreover, the researchers stated that the emotional brain experiences difficulty when visualizing the future, even though the logical brain is able to pinpoint the possible consequences of present actions. People who let their emotional brains rule are not able to recognize the possible future benefits of waiting.

Case Studies of Top Performers

Morten Hansen wrote Great at Work: How Top Performers Do Less, Work Better and Achieve More. In his book, he presented a case study that focused on skill mastery. However, instead of the traditional

10,000 hours, he claimed that it only takes half of that time to master a particular skill.

According to him, the world's top performers use this technique so that they can achieve maximum result with the least effort. After getting his Master's degree, he got a job at the Boston Consulting Group. There, he noticed that one of his colleagues worked fewer hours and yet still produced better results than him. He became curious as to how this could happen when they have the same work experience.

Hansen went on to get more credentials and eventually landed a teaching position at the University of California, Berkeley. During his time there as a professor, he looked back on his experience at Boston Consulting Group and started to research. He studied about five thousand subjects in five years.

He co-authored the book Great by Choice in 2011. He talked about the frameworks of outstanding performance. He said that people can improve their work performance if they employ the seven "work-smart practices". The first four practices are about mastering your work while the rest are about mastering the way you work with other people.

What Do Top Performers Have In Common?

The most successful people often make the most contribution to organizations. In fact, researchers have found that 10% of a company's productivity is caused by the top 1% of employees. Likewise, 26% of the output comes from the top 5%.

This means that the cream of the crop produces four times as much as average employees. Major companies, such as Google and Apple, even have bigger gaps between their high performers and average workers. They are highly successful because they employ the best people.

So, what sets high performers apart from the rest of the crowd? In a survey of one thousand employers, the following are said to be reasons why high performers stand out:

Top performers share similar attributes.

In general, high performers are great problem solvers. They are driven and self-directed. They also possess initiative and strategic thinking skills. They are motivated to get things done, even without much supervision and assistance. They often go to great lengths just to produce a great output.

Top performers combine learned skills with innate talents.

The best innate qualities, according to employers, are self-direction, initiative, and drive. Top performers possess these qualities. Then, they learn skills such as problem solving and strategic thinking. They are individuals who have an innate bias towards action as well as the capability to learn how to execute tasks effectively.

CHAPTER 6

HOW TO USE VISUALIZATION TECHNIQUE TO GET THINGS DONE

A lot of people are not aware of the powers of visualization. This is why they are not able to maximize it for their benefit. Also, a lot of people practice visualization the wrong way. Instead of visualizing the life that they want, they visualize the life that they do not want.

For example, they let their doubts, fears, and worries get the best of them. So, instead of pursuing something that might lead to a good outcome, they hesitate and stop before they even begin.

In addition, there is a common misconception that visualization is only for people who do not live in reality. The truth, however, is that people who practice visualization are aware of the positivity that the technique can bring into their lives.

For example, Olympic athletes practice visualization to do well in sports. This actually applies to both adults and children. In studies done at the Beijing Institute of Physical Education as well as the University of Ottawa, the researchers found that young table tennis players between 7 and 10 years old were able to perform better when they practiced visualization.

Even better, visualization can have a positive impact on your physical state. In a study done by exercise psychologist Guang Yue at the Cleveland Clinic Foundation in Ohio, it was found that individuals who performed virtual workouts in three months were able to boost their muscle strength by 13.5%. Simply imagining that they were working out made them stronger and better than 30% of those who actually worked out.

Benefits of Visualization

When you practice visualization on a regular basis, you can reap the following benefits:

a. Visualization will activate your creative subconscious mind, which generates ideas that you can use to attain your objective.

b. Visualization will program your brain so that it can easily recognize and perceive the resources that you need to achieve your goals.

c. Visualization will activate the law of attraction and help you attract the right people, situations, and resources.

d. Visualization will build your internal motivation so that you will be prompted to take the right actions.

Different Visualization Techniques

The essence of visualization is imagining yourself improving, succeeding, and getting what you want. A basic visualization technique requires nothing more than simply sitting in a peaceful location, closing your eyes, and visualizing good things. However, there are also other visualization techniques that you can try.

The Mental Rehearsal Technique

As you have read earlier in this chapter, athletes often practice visualization before a competition to improve their performance. Specifically, they practice mental rehearsal, which is an exercise that was popularized in the 1960's by the Russians.

Each day, they set aside several minutes to practice this technique. The most ideal times are after waking up, after practicing meditation, and before going to bed. It is during these times that your mind and body are most relaxed. Here are the steps:

Step 1. Visualize yourself sitting inside a dark movie theater. After a brief moment, the movie begins to play on the screen. It is a movie about you. In this movie, you are your best self and you have the life that you have always wanted.

When you visualize the movie about your life, make sure that you cover everything, from what you are wearing to how your hair is styled. Take note of your facial expressions and body language. Don't forget to visualize your surroundings and the people around you, if there are any.

You can even include sounds such as music, traffic noise, chirping of birds, chattering of passersby, etc. Make your visualization as realistic and detailed as possible. More importantly, make sure that you embody the feelings that you believe you would experience when you get your desired results.

Step 2. Visualize yourself getting up from your seat and walking towards the screen. You open a secret door in the screen and you step inside into the movie. Now, you can experience the entire thing once more. This time, however, you are looking out through your own eyes.

This is referred to as embodied image. It strengthens the effect of the experience. Once again, make sure that you visualize everything in detail and embody the feelings that you expect to have.

Step 3. Finally, you should visualize yourself getting out of the movie screen and going back to your seat. Look at the screen as it continues to play your wonderful life. Then, reach for it and reduce its size with your hands. Once it becomes as small as a piece of cracker, pop it inside your mouth and chew it. Chew it carefully and swallow.

Imagine that every morsel contains a detail about your life. Visualize these tiny pieces going from your mouth down to your stomach, and then towards the different cells in your body. Imagine your cells lighting up with the movie about your perfect life.

This exercise usually takes about five minutes to do. When you are done, you can open your eyes again and get through the rest of your day.

Creating Goal Pictures

This technique is about creating a mental picture of yourself achieving your goal. For example, if your goal is to buy a new car, you can have your picture taken with a new car. If your goal is to go to Paris, you can Photoshop your picture with an image of the Eiffel Tower. Essentially, you have to visualize yourself and the affirmation of your goal.

Step 1. Think of a goal that you have always wanted.

Step 2. Get a physical picture that represents or reflects this goal.

Step 3. Allow the image to influence your life until you eventually attain your goal.

Just think of the authors of Chicken Soup for the Soul. Before their first book became a hit, they were only hoping that it would be on the New York Times bestseller list. They scanned a copy of this list and inserted the title of their book.

So, it looked like Chicken Soup for the Soul was actually the top selection in the Paperback Advice,

How-To and Miscellaneous category. They also printed several copies and placed them all over the office.

About a couple of years later, their visualization became a reality. Chicken Soup for the Soul was a bestseller. It actually got the top spot in that category. Today, the book is still very popular amongst readers of all ages.

Index Cards

You can also write your goals on index cards. This way, you can take them with you when you travel. Staying away from home should not be a reason for you to forget about your goals.

Step 1. Get some 3 x 5 index cards.

Step 2. Write down your goals on the index cards. Keep them near you so that you can quickly reach for them whenever necessary. For example, you can store them in your bedside table.

Step 3. Every morning and evening, you should get the index cards and read your goals. This way, you will be reminded of them. Get one card. Close your eyes for fifteen seconds. Visualize yourself achieving the goal written on this card.

Step 4. Open your eyes. Get another index card and repeat the process until you are done practicing visualization with all the cards.

How to Use Visualization to Get the Results that You Desire

This visualization technique is highly effective for overcoming procrastination. You just have to visualize yourself starting and finishing your tasks as well as achieving your goals.

For example, if you want to be a published author, you can visualize yourself starting to draft an outline for your book, writing the chapters, and getting the book published.

To help you practice visualization correctly, here are the steps that you have to follow:

Step 1. Have a clear idea of what you want.

You have to define what you want and why you want it. Otherwise, you will not be able to visualize and manifest whatever it is that you hope to achieve. Have a clear understanding of what you value as well as what brings you the most joy. Recall any moments in which you felt genuinely joyful. What were you doing during that time? This may give you an idea of what you truly want in life.

Step 2. Describe your vision in vivid details.

In order to turn your visions into reality, such visions have to be accurate and complete. You can write down your visualization and include all the necessary details. You can also put together pictures and create a vision board. When you have a clear vision of what you want, it will be much easier for you to achieve it.

Step 3. Begin to visualize and feel the emotions that come along.

When you are ready, you may pause for a while and begin to visualize the result that you wish to achieve. Begin to visualize everything, from the scenery to the scent to the sound. As you visualize, make sure that you also feel the emotions that are connected to this new reality. Ask yourself what you would feel if your visualizations really happen.

Step 4. Take action every single day.

The key to success is continuity. You cannot start something and stop abruptly. You have to continue doing it until you get better at it. You have to keep going until you achieve your desired outcome.

So, if you want your visualizations to come true, you have to take action every day. Continue to work towards your goal and avoid getting caught up with your distance. Focus on your present but do not forget to set short term goals that you have to target daily, weekly, or monthly.

Step 5. Persevere and have grit.

Challenges and problems are natural parts of life. Even the most successful people experience hardships at some point. The key to succeeding is persevering and having grit.

When you practice visualization, you have to imagine yourself overcoming obstacles and challenges. Imagine yourself courageously facing them instead of hiding or running away. Determine whatever it is that can help you persevere in the face of adversities.

Visualization is ideal to be paired with affirmations. So, aside from imagining yourself achieving your goals, you should also give yourself positive self-talk. Tell yourself repeatedly that you are worthy of the good things that you want in life and that you are capable of achieving them.

The combination of visualization and affirmation actually harnesses eighteen billion cells in your brain. Thus, your brain is able to work in a purposeful and singular direction. It will also engage your subconscious mind so that you can be trained to stay optimistic in spite of adversities.

CHAPTER 7

THE IMPORTANCE OF TAKING ACTION

Studying theories is great. It lets you learn about many different things. However, learning about these theories is not enough. You also have to put them into action. You have to experiment and test your hypotheses. This way, you can find out if what you think is accurate or factual.

With regard to procrastination, reading about the strategies on how to overcome it is not enough. You actually have to apply these strategies in your day-to-day life.

Actions activate facts or data.

Nothing will change if no action is taken. What do you think will change after you watch a motivational video or read a self-help book? Nothing will change unless you take the necessary actions.

For example, if you want to raise your self-confidence level, you can watch a motivational video or read a how-to article. This will give you inspiration as well as let you know what you have to do.

Afterwards, make sure that you do not just sit around. Get up and take action. Apply the lessons that you have just watched or read into your life. Simply watching videos and reading articles will not magically transform you into a whole new person. You have to combine your vision with action.

Actions facilitate the elimination method.

Without taking action, you will not be able to know which tips or techniques do not work. In order for you to verify the reliability of anything, you have to test or try it out for yourself.

Try to do the various strategies or techniques that you have read. Ideally, you should write them down so that you will not get confused. Cross out the ones that you do not find helpful or effective.

Actions create habits, which eventually yields success.

The more you do something, the more it gets ingrained into your system. Eventually, it becomes automatic.

For example, if you want to be a professional tennis player, you should do what you have to do. You can start by reading books about tennis and compiling your research. You can also watch tennis matches on TV and online.

Then, you have to get out there and practice playing tennis. You can hire a coach or invite your friends to play with you. Make sure that you play tennis at the same time every day. This way, your new habit will become automatic.

Actions stop complaints.

It is typical for people to complain about something. Sadly, they are mostly just talk. They do not do anything to get the results that they want.

For example, if you want to take a nap, but your neighbor is playing loud music, what would you do? If you choose to complain, you will not get anywhere. This is especially true if you live somewhere far and you are isolated from your family and friends.

Rather than murmur complaints and become bitter, you should take the necessary actions. In this case, you can walk to your neighbor's house and knock on their door. Then, you should politely ask them if they can turn down their music because you are trying to sleep.

Actions Overcome Fears

Your fears can take over your life if you do not do anything about them. For example, if you want to expand your social circle, you should go out and meet new people. You can attend parties, events, and other social gatherings.

While this may sound fun, it can also be quite fearful. After all, going out of your comfort zone means that you have to take risks. You may be rejected, embarrassed, hurt, etc. Doing something new can overwhelm you.

Nevertheless, not doing anything is worse than taking the risk. If you do not take action, you will always wonder what could have happened if you put yourself out there. You will be regretful of your decision to stay in your comfort zone.

CHAPTER 8

TIME

MANAGEMENT

Time is an extremely vital resource because it cannot be stored or saved for later use. Thus, you have to make the most of the time that you have. You have to learn how to manage time wisely so that you can be productive and efficient.

Importance and Benefits of Time Management

Time management is essential because it helps you get things done. It helps increase productivity, identify priorities, and make conscious decisions with regard to spending time on valuable activities and tasks.

Without proper time management, your life can be a mess. You will not know which things you have to do first, as well as how you can finish everything on time. It will prevent you from making any progress.

So, if you want to gain balance in your life, you have to manage your time wisely. Effective time management helps you save energy, have more creativity, and stay on the right track.

When you are able to manage your time properly, you will be more punctual and disciplined. You will also be more organized. Rather than do things spontaneously, you will follow a specific route or plan. You will have a schedule for meetings, presentations, hobbies, dates, and other activities. Hence, you will be able to do everything you want, without having to sacrifice certain aspects of your life.

A lot of people believe that it is not possible to have it all. They think that they have to sacrifice certain things for other things because their time is limited. For example, a woman in her 30's may think that she can no longer pursue post-graduate studies because she has to focus on raising a family. She may think that there is not enough time for both her studies and family life.

However, there is actually a way to have everything you want. If you are a woman in your 30's, you can balance your personal and professional lives. You just have to create a schedule and stick with it. You should also identify your priorities and goals.

So, if you want to start a family and study for a Master's degree at the same time, you have to eliminate unnecessary activities and events on your calendar. This does not mean that you have to sacrifice certain areas of your life. It simply means that you have to get rid of unproductive and time-wasting activities, such as spending hours on social media.

You can pursue your post-graduate studies and still have time to date or go out with friends. Your social life does not have to suffer just because you want to meet a prospective partner to start a family with as well as get a Master's degree.

Furthermore, effective time management improves your planning and forecasting skills. You will be able to plan things in the most efficient ways as well as know where they may stand in the future.

On the other hand, ineffective time management can result in problems. It can make you miss deadlines, produce low quality results, or get stressed. It can even damage your personal and professional relationships. For example, if you are often late, others may find you unreliable or lazy.

The Action Priority Matrix

It can help you determine which tasks are urgent and important. It organizes tasks into different categories.

In order for you to make the action priority matrix work, you have to score your activities depending on how they affect you.

The ones that have a high impact and require low effort are Quick Wins. These are your best tasks or activities because they give you huge returns for minimal efforts.

The ones that have a high impact and require high effort are Major Projects. They also yield good returns. However, they consume too much time and energy.

The ones that have a low impact and require low effort are Fill Inns. They are not that important. So, you can opt to do them at a later time.

Finally, the ones that have a low impact and require high effort are Thankless Tasks. They yield little return yet they consume a lot of time and energy. They should be avoided, as much as possible.

The Time Management Matrix

It was created by Stephen Covey, author of the popular book The 7 Habits of Highly Effective People. It allows you to schedule your activities based on their importance and urgency. It consists of four quadrants, which you can use to determine which tasks you have to prioritize.

Quadrant I is also known as the Quadrant of Necessities. It consists of tasks that are both urgent and important. Thus, they have to be done right away.

Quadrant II is also known as the Quadrant of Quality. It consists of tasks that are important but not urgent. Hence, you have to do them, but there is no need for you to rush. These tasks are proactive and can improve the quality of your life.

Quadrant III is also known as the Quadrant of Deception. It consists of tasks that are urgent but not important. They can waste your time and drain your energy. So, you can minimize or eliminate them completely.

Quadrant IV is also known as the Quadrant of Waste. It consists of tasks that are both not urgent and not important. They do not really make your life better. So, you can opt to not do them at all.

Effective Time Management Techniques

The following are time management techniques that have been proven to be easy and effective:

Set your priorities straight.

What are the things that you have to do? These are the things that absolutely have to be done if you do not want to experience unpleasant consequences. You can create a list of your tasks and then cross out the ones that may be delegated or eliminated.

Set a timeframe for your tasks.

When you have a specific schedule, you will be less inclined to procrastinate. Ideally, you should print out your schedule and stick it on your dresser mirror, computer monitor, or refrigerator door. This way, you will always be reminded of the tasks that you have to finish as well as how long you should allot for each task.

Keep things organized.

People are more likely to procrastinate if they live in a messy environment. So, you should organize your things. Place them in cabinets, shelves, drawers, and other storage locations. When you have a clean workspace, you will find it much easier to move around and search for items. More importantly, you will be more motivated to complete your task.

Plan your day ahead.

You should also plan your week, month, and year ahead. However, you should begin with just one day. Once you are able to get through this day, you will be motivated to get through the other days. What are the things that you have to accomplish for the day? Make sure that you include them in your schedule.

CONCLUSION

I'd like to thank you and congratulate you for transiting my lines from start to finish.

I hope this book was able to help you learn about procrastination and what commonly causes it. I hope that it was also able to motivate you to take the right actions.

More importantly, I hope that I was able to help you get started on your journey towards success. If you follow the tips given in this book, you will surely be able to stay on the right track.

Keep in mind that it is never too late to make a change. No matter how much procrastination you have done in the past, you can always turn your life around and make positive changes.

The next step is to apply the lessons that you have learned from this book into your life. Start by performing the exercises to boost productivity and overcome procrastination.

I wish you the best of luck!

BONUS

CHAPTER

MENTAL TOUGHNESS

CHAPTER 1

Plato in his "Republic" talks about mental discipline. The Romans believed that men had to study certain subjects in order to become trained in the best traits of life which included basic intelligence, the right attitude towards things as well as core values. The subjects the Romans believed could bring about this type of mental fortitude were music, geometry, grammar, logic, astronomy, rhetoric and arithmetic. In Greco-Roman times these subjects were studied by rote and imitation. This lasted until quite recently and it was only later when pedagogues decided that this type of education was counter-productive and what was required was a "softer" type of education based on moral values and the humanities studies were brought to the fore, however, we will not deal with this and will deal with the basics about mental discipline which in our times is seeing a resurgence in modern thinking.

Today mathematics is seen to be a mental discipline and the idea is to transpose mathematical thinking to common life thinking and problem solving.

One of the ways to achieve mental discipline is to use mindfulness. This is a type of thinking that means we focus on what we are doing right now down to the finest detail. For example; eating. In mindfulness we would focus first on the table. Look at the table, see what its colours are, if it is wood, glass, iron or plastic. How high the table is. What it measures. What is on the table. The cutlery we are going to use to eat, the dishes, the different sets of dishes and cutlery for the other people that will be eating with us. Then we focus on the food. What exactly are we going to be eating. How we will be eating and we focus on our body, our arm reaching for the fork, the hand that grasps the fork, the fingers that hold it, the hand that goes down reaching for the food, the morsel that is placed on the fork. How the fingers, hand, arm and body move as we place the fork in our mouth with the food. The food. Is it hot or cold? Is it crunchy or soft? Does it drip. Is it salty or sweet? The colour of it. The odour of it. We chew it carefully extracting all the nutrition in it. We swallow. We focus all the time on the act of eating and we eat carefully, being and fusing ourselves with the act of nutrition. We are not distracted by other people, tv, a book, the radio, etc. We focus on the act of eating single minded. This is mindfulness and it can be applied to everything we do. By practicing mindfulness every day, we can reinforce our willpower and according to scientists, this can actually increase gravy matter in the brain.

Willpower is strengthened by mindfulness. Willpower is about the refusal to give in, to cave. Willpower is mindfulness in action. By meditating you create a calm space in your mind where your mind is not leaping from one thing to the next and with willpower you force your mind to stay still in the present. This is not easy. You must have tried meditating from time to time and all it did was two things: you got restless and left the meditation room or else you fell asleep. The way to meditate is to use mindfulness to calm your mind and anchor it to the present. Try to sit still and pay attention to what is happening around you or in you at this precise moment. Don´t get distracted. Just sit there and focus on what is happening right now. It is hard. Mental discipline is about doing this every single time you lose focus and this is where willpower comes in. Willpower is what will get you where you want to be every time your attention wanes. The best thing about willpower is that it can be fortified just like your mind because it is like a muscle and you can make it stronger.

Willpower is part of self-discipline. It is the essence of self-discipline. Forcing yourself to do things cannot be done without willpower. Willpower is the grease that the self-discipline machine uses to carry out the motions leading you to a better place inside yourself.

Willpower is what you need to strengthen in order to have mental discipline, it is one of the ingredients you need on your way to a more disciplined mind.

So, we have some things to use now right at the very beginning: mindfulness which is a form of willpower in baby steps. Willpower and these are attitudinal things that we need to use in our quest for mental discipline.

How do we get mental discipline?

There is no easy way to obtain mental discipline. It takes a lifetime to cultivate the mind. It is almost an art (remember the music, one of the subjects of the Romans that Plato talked about?). There is no way to buy yourself mental discipline. The only way is hard work so prepare for that. Make yourself a plan, a scheme, a way to tackle the issue. Use a notebook to write down all the things you will be doing and keep a sort of mental discipline diary. Read it every day.

Maybe you had a falling out in life, maybe something derailed you from your set path you had. Now while you are in your low moment, or contemplative moment, is the time to set the groundwork for your future which starts now (remember, mindfulness). Now is the time to ditch the old you that wasn't working and get yourself a new you (remember, attitudes). Make yourself abide by a new set of rules. There are ways in which you can use your daily living activities to have more self-discipline. One is getting up early. This doesn't seem like much but if you include it in your new you, it will make you start the day at a different hour and this in itself is going to have an impact on your day. Try it, if you get up at 8 in the morning, try getting up at 7 and see what the world looks like at that time of day. At first you will need almost all your willpower because when you open your eyes and see that it is still very early, your body will be begging you to snuggle down and stay in bed. Don´t. Get up and take a shower. Get yourself a coffee and once you have overcome the temptation to stay in bed and are actually in the kitchen preparing a coffee or a juice, give yourself a pat on the back. It will get easier as your mind adapts to your new schedule and, now that you have gotten up, what about using this extra hour for something special? Try meditation. Go into your living room or your porch with your coffee. If it is summer, sit out there in mindfulness taking in the sensations of the early morning. Stay out there for an hour, it won´t be wasted. Remember, you are rewarding yourself for having gotten up early and you got up early because you are on your way to having greater mental discipline. You are mapping out the steps you need to achieve your long-term goal and don´t forget to keep the forest in mind while focusing on the trees. This is a sample of what a person can do in an easy way to change his or her life.

Mental discipline is something you can learn but it is necessary to practice and repeat it a lot. This is the downside but if you use mindfulness as a tool, you can practice and repeat endlessly and effortlessly after a while because with mindfulness every time you do it is like the first time and this comes with an added thing, a Zen like quality that makes repetition pleasurable. If you practice a sport you will know what this is: it is hitting the ball perfectly every time like in tennis or the runner's "high", the surge of dopamine in the brain helping you overcome the grind of repetition. If you make it a habit to observe yourself in a detached way while you are doing your practicing and repetition, you will develop your mindfulness and your self-discipline. There are ways that can help you achieve your self-discipline. One thing is to make it easy on yourself, eliminate things that suck your energy, that detract from your goal, for example, if you were dieting, eliminate the snacks and junk food. This is just common sense. It is not a good idea to go to the supermarket at lunch time. Use your common sense and eliminate the temptations that are going to undermine your self-discipline. If you get up in the morning early, do it. Get up and get away from the bed. Move. Go to the kitchen. Do something so you don't crawl back into bed.

While considering snacks and junk food, remember to focus on healthy eating. This is part of the Spartan like training you will need to foster your mental-discipline so take it to another level and include proper eating in your routine.

Another element in getting mental discipline is to give yourself prizes for achieving things. Don't make your quest for mental discipline a Marine training site because you will make things so difficult, so almost impossible to achieve that you will fail. Set yourself easy to achieve goals, gradually make them a little harder and set yourself up to win. This is a difficult thing. Lots of people who have decided to embark on achieving mental discipline to immure them from failure and disappointment do so because they have suffered a lot from failure and disappointment. One of the things to watch out for is the paradoxical thing which is: I fasted for one day and didn´t eat anything. I am great. Then, immediately after, I rush out to McDonalds and have a binge… Why is this? This is because my mental discipline is so green and raw that I cannot withstand success and need to fail. Then we feel miserable and get all despondent and start considering Spartan discipline… this is wrong. The thing to do is to take it in stride.

Make room for failure and remember to immediately get up and start again or rather, continue. This is the key word: continue. The first time you have a major fail, you will throw this book out the window and go to bed feeling miserable because you failed. But if you go out and find this book and dust it off and read it again, the next time you fail will not be as bad. And this is the wonderful thing. Failing starts fading. Winning starts pushing failing to a side and one day during your mindfulness you will notice how you have changed.

Change: This is the secret to staying young forever. Change. The way in which you no longer do the things you used to do and now do new things or different ones. These are things to consider. If you let yourself change. If you are flexible and use your failings to change yourself, you will find ways in which your mental discipline will start having an effect on what you do every day. Experience is mindfulness in action. Mindfulness is mental discipline in action.

When you fail, which you will do, be sure to take note. Be disappointed, frustrated and angry but don't forget the forest while you bash your head against the tree. Keep the forest in mind and go back. Get up early and dedicate some early morning silence to mindfulness and pick up where you left off. Practice makes perfect and remember, the Greco-Romans prided themselves on rote learning. So you should too.